The Devon Beach and Cove Guide

Robert Hesketh

Bossiney Books · Launceston

First published 2010 by Bossiney Books Ltd
Langore, Launceston, Cornwall PL15 8LD
www.bossineybooks.com
ISBN 978-1-906474-18-8

Acknowledgements
The maps on pages 12 and 29 are by Graham Hallowell,
that on page 4 by Nick Hawken
All photographs are by the author or from the publishers' own collection

Printed in Great Britain by R Booth Ltd, Penryn, Cornwall

Introduction

Devon's two coasts provide over 225km (140 miles) of remarkably varied natural beauty. Whether you're looking for swimming, surfing, scenery, watersports or just lazing in the sun, a traditional beach resort or a Robinson Crusoe experience, this guide is designed to help you find what you want. Practical information, including parking, access and lifeguard cover, as well as facilities such as beach cafés, shops and toilets are given to help you choose from over 100 beaches and coves around the county. Each one is illustrated.

Beach safety

Devon's beaches are delightful and safe places – provided beach users take responsibility for their own safety and follow a few simple common sense precautions, especially with children. Tides and currents affect all beaches, but some much more than others. Please check tide times, heed warning notices and keep well within the limits of your strength and skill. Surfing and other water sports require specialist knowledge.

Avoid swimming or boating alone or in rough seas. Take notice of warnings of dangerous currents. Do not swim if the red flag is flying or in zones covered by the black and white flag (watercraft only). On lifeguarded beaches, swim between the red/yellow flags. Some beaches have first aid facilities, telephones or lifeguard cover in the summer months. In emergency, call the Coastguard on 999.

Other potential hazards that can be readily avoided include being cut off on isolated beaches by the tide; drifting out to sea on inflatable boats (never use them if the orange windsock is flying: it indicates offshore winds); slipping on wet rocks (wear shoes); and tunnelling deeply into soft sand, which can collapse.

On certain beaches, mainly in East Devon and Torbay (where beaches occasionally have to be closed), rock falls are a potential hazard but only directly under unstable cliffs. Please heed warning notices. Equally, keep away from cliff edges if exploring the Coast Path.

Seashore code

Please do your bit towards protecting Devon's wonderful coasts.
   Take litter home.
   Return all live specimens – crabs, prawns etc – to the water.
   Replace seaweeds and rocks where you find them.
   Report anything unusual.

Key to symbols used

P	Parking
P	Free parking (at the time of writing)
WC	Toilets
⌂	Sandy beach
⌖	Surfing popular – but not necessarily safe!
⌿	Water-skiing
⌁	Snorkelling
⚑	Lifeguards (seasonal only)
✚	First aid
🐕	Dogs banned (sometimes summer only)
🐕	Dogs permitted all year (at the time of writing)
✗	Café
⛾	Pub or bar fairly near
🏠	Shop(s)
🦅	Wildlife
🐟	Fishing
📞	Public telephone (other than emergency phone)

Coastal Tourist Information Centres

Barnstaple 01271 375000	Kingsbridge 01548 853195
Bideford 01237 477676	Lynton 01598 752225
Braunton 01271 816400	Plymouth 01752 304849
Budleigh Salterton 01395 445275	Salcombe 01548 843927
	Seaton 01297 21660
Combe Martin 01271 883319	Sidmouth 01395 516441
Dartmouth 01803 834224	Shaldon 01626 873723
Dawlish 01626 215665	Teignmouth 01626 215666
Exmouth 01395 222299	Torbay 01803 211211
Ilfracombe 01271 863001	Woolacombe 01271 870553

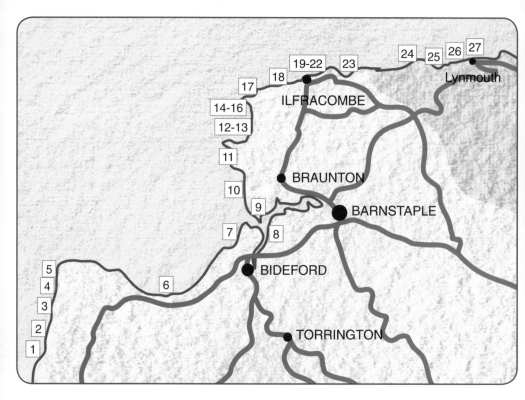

North Devon beaches

Devon's north coast is remarkably different from the Channel coast. It divides naturally into three parts.

The rugged coast between the Cornish border and Hartland Point, where the wild Atlantic meets the Bristol Channel, has a character all its own, with surf-washed stretches of saw-toothed rocks beneath towering cliffs of contorted rock cut by waterfalls: these beaches are great places to find solitude and inspirational scenery.

Devon's best surfing, as well as sports from sandcastling to sail-boarding, can be enjoyed on the golden sandy beaches between West-ward Ho! and Morte Point. Extensive dunes at Braunton, Saunton and Croyde shelter a remarkable variety of plants and animals – please ex-plore carefully to help protect these unique environments.

East of Morte Point, the beaches are quite different again, a mix of sand, shingle and rock. Some are popular with families. The more re-mote coves, guarded by spectacular whale-backed cliffs that rise to over 300m along the Exmoor coast, call for exploration on foot.

1 Marsland Mouth

A beautiful and secluded rocky beach amid dramatic cliff scenery and washed by powerful Atlantic waves. It requires a tough 1km walk to reach and has no facilities. Enjoy solitude, sea and birds, beware crumbling cliffs and rock falls.

2 Welcombe Mouth

At high tide the surf roars over the pebbles at Welcombe; as the tide drops, long rocky ridges and a little sand appear. High cliffs and a pretty waterfall add to Welcombe's charm. Access is by a short, steep path from the car park, itself reached by a narrow lane and a rough track.

3 Speke's Mill Mouth

A 1.25km (1 mile) walk leads to a dramatic beach of pebbles and saw toothed rocks, great for contemplation, rock pooling and exercising a dog. Low tide reveals some sand too. Park at Hartland Quay and follow the Coast Path south for 1.25km (1 mile) and then take the steep path – near the waterfall, the largest on the Coast Path – down to the beach.

4 Hartland Quay

Low tide reveals a beautiful if rugged beach of rocks, pebbles and some sand beneath Hartland's spectacular cliffs. Easily accessible from the slipway at Hartland Quay, which has ample parking and a range of facilities including a pub/hotel, the beach has rock pools for children and waves for surfing.

5 Blegberry

Like Hartland Quay and Speke's Mill Mouth, Blegberry is a beach of pebbles and rocks with some sand at low tide, backed by splendid rock formations with waterfalls. It has no facilities and is accessible only from the Coast Path, a 20 minute hike from Hartland Quay.

🐕 For parking and facilities see Hartland Quay above.

6 Buck's Mills

Buck's Mills is a pretty village. Reached by a 650 m walk from a free car park, its rocky beach has a waterfall and a fine vista of Bideford Bay, plus much of historical interest. There is a disused lime-kiln perched on the cliff, rusting winches on the sea wall and the remains of the quay. Sports fishing and some commercial fishing continues. There's a shop at Buck's Cross.

7 Westward Ho!

A vast beach of sand and surf. Westward Ho! developed as a Victorian family resort and has amusements, cafés and pubs aplenty. Beach buggies, boogie boards, deckchairs and windbreaks can all be hired. The northern (Sandymere, photo bottom left) end of the beach is known for surfing and is approached from Northam Burrows car park. In Westward Ho! itself parking can be a problem in high season. Dogs banned May-Sept.

8 Instow

Popular with both families and sailors. It has a clean, attractive, gently sloping beach of golden sand and shallow water to swim in. Protected by Bideford Bar, the Taw/Torridge estuary is ideal for sailing and windsurfing. Instow is HQ of the North Devon Yacht Club and Appledore Lifeboat station is only minutes away. Disabled access.

P WC ⛺ 🐕 🏠 🍴 🍷 📞

9 Crow Point

An excellent place to relax and explore Braunton Burrows (see below), Crow Point is at the quieter end of Saunton Sands, where the Taw/Torridge estuary meets the sea. Approach via the toll road from Braunton.

P ⛺ 🐕 🐦 🎣

10 Saunton Sands

5km of golden sands washed by rolling waves ideal for surfing, it has space and scope for a range of beach activities. Behind the sands are Braunton Burrows, 1000 hectares of dunes supporting an amazing diversity of wildflowers and birds. Dogs 🐕 in certain areas.

P WC ⛺ 🏄 🏓 🏠 🍴 🐦

11 Croyde

Croyde has good facilities and a fine stretch of sand backed by dunes. One of Devon's leading surfing beaches, it is popular with families, but notices warn of rip tides and undercurrents. Several watersports, including jet skis, windsurfing and kitesurfing are not allowed.

P WC ⛺ 🏄 🏓 ➕ 🐕 🏠 🍴 🍷 📞

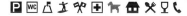

12 Putsborough Sand

The quieter southern end of 3km long Woolacombe Sand, this is a beautiful beach of golden sand and surf, making it popular with families and beach boys alike. Well managed by a local family firm, it has good facilities. Dogs banned from part of beach. Access by steps.

🅿 🆆 ⛺ 🏊 🤸 ➕ 🐴 🏠 🍴 📞

13 Woolacombe Sands

Woolacombe's huge sandy beach is justifiably one of the most popular in Devon. A magnet for surfers, it also draws families. Divided into three zones to accommodate various users and sports, Woolacombe Sands is carefully managed and watched by lifeguards. It has something to offer all visitors, plus a comprehensive range of facilities. Dogs: limited ban (🐕 in Zone C, 🐕 on leads in Zone B and 🐕 April to November in Zone A).

🅿 🆆 ⛺ 🏊 🤸 ➕ 🏠 🍴 🍷 📞

14 Barricane Beach

Very similar to, but separate from, neighbouring Coombesgate Beach though without enough room for surfing. Limited roadside parking. Dogs 🐕 on a lead only April-Sept.

🅿 ⛺ 🏠 🍴

15 Coombesgate Beach

A beach of golden sand, popular with surfers and families alike. If you can find convenient roadside parking, access is moderately short, but involves steps. Shop and café at neighbouring Barricane.

⛺ 🏊

16 Grunta Beach

A small beach of rocks and coarse sand with beautiful views of Morte Point, accessible by a ten minute walk and a steep path from Mortehoe, which has good facilities. Interesting rock pools at low tide

17 Rockham Beach, Mortehoe

A fairly demanding but very scenic 1.5 km (1 mile) walk from Mortehoe is rewarded by Rockham's beautiful beach of rocky ridges and sand with lots of rock pools. Rockham has no facilities, but there is a good range in Mortehoe. Beware rock falls.

18 Lee Bay

Lee Bay is sheltered by dramatic cliffs of folded slate and backed by a pretty village with a craft centre and a noted inn cum post office that offers cream teas. The easily accessed beach of rocks, shingle and sand has interesting rock pools at low tide. There are attractive coves to the right but don't get cut off by the tide.

19 Tunnels Beaches, Ilfracombe

As well as being an attractive stretch of sand and rocks with good facilities, including a seawater pool, they are a piece of social history and a key part of Ilfracombe's development as a seaside resort – tunnels cut between 1819 and 1823 – and the historic home of rock-pooling. Modest entry charge. Deckchairs and kayaks to rent.

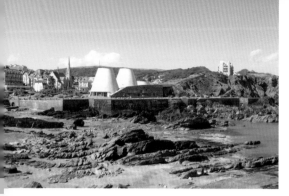

20 Wildersmouth (Ilfracombe)

A small beach of sand and rocks, Wildersmouth is conveniently situated right by Ilfracombe's Landmark and is very accessible

21 Hele Beach

An easily accessible beach of sand and shingles, Hele shelves gently and has good rock pools. Popular with families, it has handy facilities. Dogs are permitted 'under control'.

22 Watermouth

An exceptionally pretty and well sheltered harbour, Watermouth is very popular with the sailing fraternity and many pleasure boats are moored here. The mud and sand beach is easily accessed by a ramp – but it's not really a place for buckets and spades. There is a shop in the neighbouring campsite.

23 Combe Martin

Surrounded by splendid rock formations and high cliffs, Combe Martin's two beaches of sand and shingle offer easy access with good facilities close to hand. Popular with families, this steeply shelving beach shows to best advantage at low tide when the rock pools are exposed. Beware rock falls.

24 Heddon's Mouth

This rocky beach is strewn with large pebbles and surrounded by dramatic cliff scenery. Heddon's Mouth is approached by a beautiful and surprisingly level 1.7 km walk along a deep and steep sided valley from Hunter's Inn, where the parking and facilities are found.

25 Woody Bay

Woody Bay's stunningly beautiful beach of sand, shingles and rocks does not draw crowds because it has no facilities and reaching it demands a steep 1.3 km walk from the car park. The western end has a waterfall, an old lime kiln and amazing rock pools. The eastern end is only accessible by scrambling over rocks – difficult and potentially dangerous, especially with a rising tide to cut you off.

26 Lee Abbey Bay

A short, moderately steep track leads to Lee Abbey's peaceful beach of sand, pebbles and rocks, well suited to family days out. Dogs banned May-Sept.

27 Lynmouth

Whilst the high cliff background is spectacular, and the harbour pretty, the two beaches are too rocky for most visitors, who prefer the riverbank and coastal paths as well as Lynmouth's other facilities. Surfing is sometimes possible, though opinion varies about its quality.

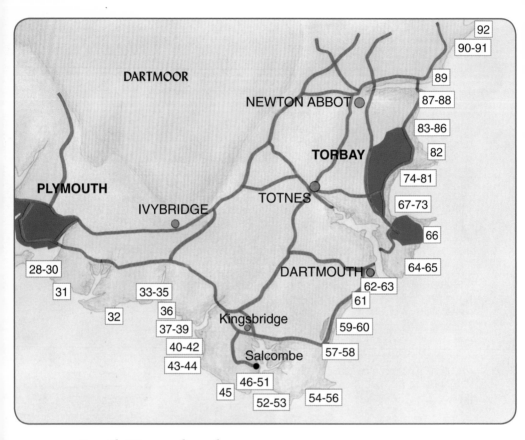

South Devon beaches

South Devon's beaches and coves provide something for everyone, from small children to water sports enthusiasts, people who enjoy convivial seaside resorts and those looking for a break from the crowds.

A mild climate and good facilities have made the sands at Paignton, Torquay, Teignmouth and Dawlish popular with families. All are on the sheltered east-facing coast, but the south- and west-facing shores have many delightful family beaches too, notably Thurlestone and South Milton Sands, Blackpool and the Salcombe estuary beaches.

Good surfing can be had on beaches open to livelier waves, including Challaborough, Bigbury and Bantham. If you're looking for somewhere less populated, South Devon has many smaller, less known beaches and coves tucked into its deeply indented coast. Finding and reaching them (often on foot and with the aid of a map) usually takes some effort, but is richly repaid with space and tranquillity.

12

28 Bovisand

Similar to neighbouring Crownhill Bay (below) and easily accessed from the same car park, Bovisand offers a good stretch of westward facing sand. Dogs are permitted here, but not at Crownhill Bay.

29 & 30 Crownhill Bay

There are two beaches here, as well as Bovisand (above). The northern beach (closest to the parking area, café/shop and toilets) is sandy with some rocks. The southern beach is rock and shingle. Both offer fine views of Plymouth Sound, Rame Head and the Breakwater.

31 Wembury

Although part gravel and shingle with some sand, Wembury is a popular family beach and noted for its abundant wildlife. The Marine Centre is open to visitors with free entry. It provides a wealth of information about the sea life of the area and runs regular rockpool rambles. Parking free to National Trust members.

32 Stoke Beach

A sandy beach with rocky outcrops, accessed from a *very* small visitors' car park by a tarred path through the holiday park and then down to the beach via steps. The nearest facilities are in Noss Mayo.

🅿 🐕

33 Mothecombe Meadowsfoot

An attractive sandy beach approached by a five minute walk from the same car park as Mothecombe's Coastguards beach (below). It is suitable for families, surfers and windsurfers alike. Please note Meadowsfoot is a private beach, only open Wednesdays and weekends.

🅿 wc ⛺ 🚶 🐕 🏠 ✕ ☎

34 Mothecombe Coastguards

This beach is huge at low tide. Mainly sand, with some shingle and rocks high up, it is well suited to windsurfing and beach games that require lots of space. Like neighbouring Meadowsfoot, it is reached by a five minute walk from the car park, but it's open all week.

🅿 wc ⛺ 🐕 🏠 ✕ ☎

35 Wonwell (Kingston)

A secluded sandy beach reached via a pretty but uneven 500 m of Coast Path from Wonwell Slipway – though at low tide, the beach is continuous between the two. To find Wonwell, follow the lane signed WONWELL BEACH from Kingston, a pretty village with a delightful inn. There is only limited parking on the verge – difficult in high season.

🅿 ⛺ 🐕 🍷

36 Ayrmer Cove

A quiet, well sheltered beach of coarse sand, the cove is approached by a pleasant, gently sloping 1 km path from the NT car park. It has no facilities, but there is a good pub at Ringmore.

37 Challaborough

A large, easily accessed sandy beach with lifeguard cover and good facilities, very popular with surfers, day visitors and guests staying in the adjacent holiday park. The shop hires out wet suits and surf boards.

38 Bigbury (Sedgewell Cove)

A long sandy beach with lifeguards and handy facilities. It is well known to surfers and also popular with families. At low tide, visitors can walk over the sand to Burgh Island, whilst a curious sea tractor provides the link at high tide. A shop hires out wet suits and surf boards. Dogs banned in season from main beach, but allowed in limited areas.

39 Bantham

Low tide makes Bantham a vast sandy beach. Popular with both families and surfers, it is backed by dunes and has lovely views of Burgh Island and the Avon estuary. Bantham village has a shop and pub, but the WC is nearby, in the car park. Dogs during season on main beach, but on estuary beach.

40 Leas Foot (Thurlestone)

A pretty, well sheltered sandy beach with rock pools, Leas Foot is a short level walk from the car park (signed from the Golf Club). Nearby Thurlestone has a pub and shop, whilst the WC is opposite the car park.

🅿 🆆 ⛺ 🐕

41 Thurlestone Sands

Thurlestone Sands forms a continuous beach with South Milton Sands (below) which has a café/kiosk, Lifeguard station and WC, but has a separate road entrance and car park. Nearby Thurlestone village has a pub and shop. Look out for birds in the wetland reserve behind the beach.

🅿 🆆 ⛺ 🪁 🐕 🍴 🐦 📞

42 South Milton Sands

South Milton Sands is the southern end of Thurlestone Sands, a long beach popular with families. South Milton has a separate road entrance, its own car park (NT), café/kiosk, Lifeguard station and WC. Confusingly, the famous holed rock or 'Thurlestone' is at the South Milton end, along with rock pools rich in marine life.

🅿 🆆 ⛺ 🪁 🐕 🍴 🐦 📞

43 Outer Hope (Mouthwell)

Outer Hope is a sheltered sandy beach with good access and very convenient facilities. Despite its small size, it had lifeguard cover at the time of writing. Dogs 🐕 on leads.

🅿 🆆 ⛺ 🪝 🪁 ✚ 🐕 🏠 🍴 🍷 📞

16

44 Inner Hope

Inner Hope forms a long, mainly sandy beach stretching to Hope's pretty little harbour at low tide. Facilities and extra parking are a short walk away at Outer Hope (above).

45 Soar Mill Cove

This small, sandy cove is well sheltered by rocks and cliffs. It is reached by a fairly gentle ten minute walk down a lane and over fields from the car park near Soar Mill Hotel (refreshments).

46 South Sands

A beautiful easily accessed stretch of golden sand, ideal for beach games and sandcastling. Salcombe's sheltered estuary is well suited to water sports of all kinds and South Sands' beach café/shop rents out kayaks, paddleboards, catamarans and wetsuits.

47 North Sands

Like nearby South Sands, a beach of golden sand, easy access and good facilities. Popular with families, it opens onto lovely views of the Salcombe estuary and Fort Charles, the last Royalist redoubt to surrender in Devon at the close of the Civil War. Dogs on leads May-Sept.

17

48 & 49 Small's Cove and Fisherman's Cove

Neighbouring beaches of golden sand with good views of Salcombe. When the tide drops they form one beach with Mill Bay. All four beaches are deservedly popular with families. Park either at Mill Bay's National Trust car park or use the small free car park at East Portlemouth and hike down the steps. Toilets at Mill Bay.

🅿 🅿 🛆 🐴 🏠 ✕

50 & 51 Mill Bay and Sunny Cove

Attractive and easily accessed sandy beaches washed by gentle estuarine waves – but please note there are undercurrents out from shore. Dogs 🐕 on leash May-Sept.

🅿 🆆🅲 🛆

52 Gara Rock

This large sandy beach is reached via a beautiful and relatively gentle ten minute walk from the parking field on the lane between Rickham and High House. (The former hotel may be replaced: there could be changes here as a result.) Enjoy the coastal views, especially from the thatched coastguard lookout.

🅿 🛆 🐕

53 Elender Cove

Hidden by jagged cliffs, Elender is a lovely small cove, with golden sand and rock pools. Walking there from Prawle Point car park takes 10-15 minutes. The path down to the beach is steep and rather tricky. Elender Cove is best at low tide and before evening shadows close in.

🅿 🐕

54 Horseley Cove

A large but little known beach of sand and rock, most interesting when low tide reveals its many rock pools. It's a 1km walk (steep in part) from East Prawle, an attractive village with a range of facilities and free parking. Take the No Through road opposite the shop/café in East Prawle. Turn left onto footpath GORAH ROCKS. Turn right onto the Coast Path towards Prawle Point and left through a metal gate to the beach.

55 Lannacombe

Reached by a narrow lane leading to a pocket-sized car park overlooking the small but pretty beach of pale sand. Low tide reveals interesting rock pools.

56 Mattiscombe

A 1km walk from Start Point car park, fairly gentle at first but steeper at the end, is rewarded by a beautiful sandy beach. Facing south, it offers a magnificent view along the cliffs to Prawle Point. To enjoy a different view and a visit to Start Point lighthouse return to the car park and follow the lane (1km).

57 North Hallsands

A quiet beach with small fishing boats winched up on the shingle; North Hallsands looks out over the great sweep of Start Bay. The seaside hamlet has been much improved since the fire-damaged hotel was replaced by tasteful new cottages.

58 Beesands

Beesands is an active fishing village, with boats pulled up on the beach, lobster and crab pots piled on the sea wall and fresh fish for sale at the café/fishmongers. A shingle beach 2km long divides the sea from the freshwater lake (a smaller version of Slapton Ley) behind. Drink in the stunning views to the lighthouse at Start Point from a table outside the Cricket Inn.

🅿 ⓦⓒ 🐕 🏠 ✕ 🍷 🦆

59 Torcross and Slapton Sands

Slapton Sands (really shingle) offers ample space, beautiful views, easy access and good facilities in both Torcross and at Slapton village. A shingle bar 4km long stretching from Torcross to beyond Strete Gate, it protects Slapton Ley – a beautiful freshwater lake noted for its birds – from the sea. Except in an easterly gale, all is peaceful now. A Sherman Tank in the Torcross car park commemorates 946 men who died in a surprise German attack during D-Day preparations in 1944, when Slapton was requisitioned for military training. Dogs and BBQs permitted on beach but please clean up afterwards.

🅿 ⓦⓒ 🔧 🐕 🏠 ✕ 🍷 🦆 🎣

60 Strete Gate

The spacious northern extension of Slapton Sands, Strete Gate is one of Britain's most beautiful and accessible nudist beaches. Discreetly distant from the road and car park, the landward side of Strete Gate's shingle ridge is a riot of pink and white valerian.

🅿 ⓦⓒ

61 Blackpool Sands

A beautiful crescent-shaped shingle beach popular with families. Very easy access. Privately owned, it is maintained to a high standard with a good range of facilities, including a licensed café and a large beach shop. These and the beach are open all year, but the attractive gardens (extra charge) only in season.

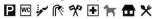

62 Deadman's Cove (Dartmouth)

This small, quiet cove is similar to adjacent Castle Cove (below), but requires a ten minute walk along the Coast Path and a long flight of steps. Facilities at Castle Cove

63 Castle Cove (Dartmouth)

Castle Cove has a small beach of gravel and rocks backed by steep cliffs. Park near Dartmouth Castle (open to the public, English Heritage) and approach via a long flight of steps.

64 Scabbacombe

A fairly demanding, but very attractive 1 km walk from Woodhuish car park leads to Scabbacombe. The effort is rewarded by a lovely quiet beach of pebbles and sand, used by both naturists and 'textiles'. There are no facilities and no restrictions.

65 Man Sands

An attractive beach of pebbles and shingle, with sand exposed at low tide, it offers a fair chance of escaping the crowds, but has no facilities. It is approached via a 1 km long stony track, steep in part and unsuitable for cars. Use the free car park at top of Woodhuish Lane.

66 St Mary's Bay (Brixham)

St Mary's is a large beach of shingle and sand, popular with families, especially those staying at the nearby holiday park. Getting there calls for a ten minute walk (involving steps) from Sharkham Point car park, which is small and thus may fill up early in the day during the high season.

67 Shoalstone Beach

A lifeguarded seawater swimming pool stands next to Shoalstone which is a shingle and rock beach, with rock pools. It is easily accessed from the car park. Dogs 🐕 except in and around the pool. Deckchairs, chalets.

68 Breakwater Beach

This is a fine place to watch the comings and goings of Brixham's delightful harbour, with its yachts and fishing boats, while enjoying splendid views across Torbay. Access from the car park is very easy and the pebbly beach has a range of facilities. Brixham's shops, cafes and pubs are a short walk away. Chalet hire and deckchairs.

69 Fishcombe Cove

Like neighbouring Churston Cove, Fishcombe is a secluded shingle and sand cove with lovely views over Torbay. It has a café/shop and toilets. Park near Battery Gardens and follow the lane as signed down to the WW2 Heritage Centre – which is small, but interesting. Turn right and downhill to the beach.

70 Churston Cove

A secluded cove without crowds or regulations, its sheltered beach of shingle and pebbles is approached in a similar way to Fishcombe Cove (above), then follow the Coast Path as signed through woods, down steps and over rocks. Facilities at Fishcombe.

71 Elberry Cove

A charming and secluded pebble cove popular with dog owners, reached by an easy ten minute walk over turf from Broadsands (below), which has the parking and other facilities lacking at Elberry.

72 Broadsands

Broadsands lives up to its name, with a broad expanse of typically red Devon sand and splendid views of Torbay. Ideal for a family day on the beach, it is easily accessed and offers a wide range of facilities. Build a sandcastle, loll in a deckchair or hire a chalet and establish a little empire by the sea. Boat and pedalo hire.

73 Goodrington

A long sandy beach with easy access and a range of facilities, from its own café, pub and shop to deckchair, boat and chalet hire. As well as good sandcastling and swimming, there is rockpooling at low tide, the Quaywest Waterpark, kiosks and amusement arcades. The free Seashore Centre has marine creatures in tanks. Dogs 🐕 on North Sands only.

🅿 ⬛ ⛺ ➕ 🏠 ✕ 🍸 📞

74 Paignton

The quintessential British popular seaside resort and ideal for children, it has a long sandy beach and a wide range of facilities. Whelks and ice cream, bouncy castles and trampolines. Deckchairs, boats and chalets can all be hired, whilst the grassy green has crazy golf and often a fun fair too. Disabled access.

🅿 ⬛ ⛺ ➕ 🐕 🏠 ✕ 🍸 ℹ

75 Preston Sands

Similar to neighbouring Paignton Sands, but without the pier. Parking is rather limited at Preston, but there is more in Paignton. Disabled access. Chalet and deckchair hire.

🅿 ⬛ ⛺ ➕ 🐕 ✕ 🍸 📞

76 Hollicombe Beach

A family friendly beach of red sand approached via gardens by Torquay Road, where there is free parking – though spaces are at a premium in the summer. Alternatively use Paignton's car parks. Rock falls closed the beach in 2009. They have been repaired, but keep clear of the cliffs and heed any warning notices.

🅿 🅿 ⬛ ⛺ 🐕

77 Livermead, Institute Beach

A small beach of coarse sand, just south of Livermead Sands and similar to it. It lacks facilities but not simple charm and is signed from the main Torquay-Paignton road, but easily missed. *Very* limited free roadside parking.

78 Livermead Sands

A pretty beach of red sand with good views across Torbay, it is best at low tide – it disappears at high tide. The middle of the beach is reserved for water skiing, but swimming is allowed elsewhere. Nearby Corbyn's beach offers a café and first aid post. Toilets are on Corbyn's Head between the two beaches. Parking is a problem.

79 Corbyn's Beach

Just south of Torre Abbey Sands, this is smaller, but enjoys the same facilities (see below). Colourful chalets give it an old fashioned air.

80 Torre Abbey Sands

A long beach of red sand, Torre Abbey Sands may be covered by the sea at the top of the tide. Washed by shallow water, it is popular with families and offers a good range of facilities, including deckchairs. Between 10 and 4 there is free roadside parking along the sea front, but if these spaces are taken Torquay has ample car parks.

81 Meadfoot Beach

A café, restaurant, water sports shop and chalets make the southern end of this shingle beach popular with families; the rockier northern end is better known to fishermen and divers. Car parks at both ends and some free roadside parking. Dogs 🐕 only at northern end. Boat, chalet and deckchair hire.

82 Anstey's Cove

A favourite haunt of Torquay-born crime writer Agatha Christie, it has a licensed café/beach shop with tables and deckchairs on the terrace. The tiny shingle beach is covered at high tide, but may be used for bathing with care. Access via a steep path from the car park.

83 Babbacombe

This pretty sand and shingle beach, backed by woods and best and sunniest in the morning, is approached by a steep lane and has a handy but small car park, which may fill in high season. Popular with divers, sailors and fishermen, who can cast from the breakwater.

84 Oddicombe Beach

Oddicombe's beautiful sand and shingle beach is approached by walking down a steep lane or by using the delightful cliff railway (1926). The far end of the beach has been closed because of rock falls. Please heed warning notices. Deckchairs, boats and chalets to hire.

85 Watcombe

A pretty, but steep woodland walk leads down to Watcombe beach, a mix of sand, shingle and pebbles which resembles Maidencombe. Well sheltered, with a reasonably priced beach café, it is popular with families. Beware rock falls.

86 Maidencombe

This is a small well sheltered sand and shingle cove, approached via steps from the car park. It benefits from a beach café and nearby pub and is popular with families. Dogs on leads. Limited free parking.

87 Shaldon Ness Beach

The Ness beach is hidden from the car park and its small zoo. Its long stretch of gently shelving sand and gravel can only be reached via a tunnel and steps cut through the distinctive headland cliff of red sandstone that guards the mouth of the Teign. Impressive lines of red cliffs stretch south to Torbay and north to Dawlish. Beware rock falls.

88 Shaldon

Connected by a foot ferry to Teignmouth beach, Shaldon beach is a strip of sand and gravel now seen, now covered by the tide. Boats galore are moored in the river, giving ever changing movement to the scene. Shaldon itself owes much of its charm to its pretty Georgian architecture, especially its inns and shops.

89 Teignmouth

A fine sandy beach and first class coastal views in a classic family seaside resort – promenade, Victorian pier, theatre and play park. Enjoy a boat trip along the coast or up the beautiful river Teign; laze in a deckchair; or explore the town, which has some good Georgian architecture. Disabled access.

90 Coryton Cove

Reached by a short, level promenade from Dawlish, with its many facilities. Well sheltered by cliffs and sea stacks of red sandstone, it is a mainly sandy beach with rockpools to explore. Disabled access.

91 Dawlish

Dawlish has a lovely sandy beach, boat trips, fishing trips and amusement arcades. Behind the beach is the park with Dawlish Water, its swans, ducks and hatchery.

92 Dawlish Warren

With a long, sandy lifeguarded beach washed by gentle currents of clear water, Dawlish Warren is an excellent family beach. It has a full range of facilities, plus amusement arcades and a fun fair. By contrast, the sandy dunes of the Warren are a nature reserve, with board walks, a visitor centre and bird watching hides, from where huge flocks of waders and sea birds are seen in winter. Dogs on main beach but on leads elsewhere. Beach huts and deckchairs.

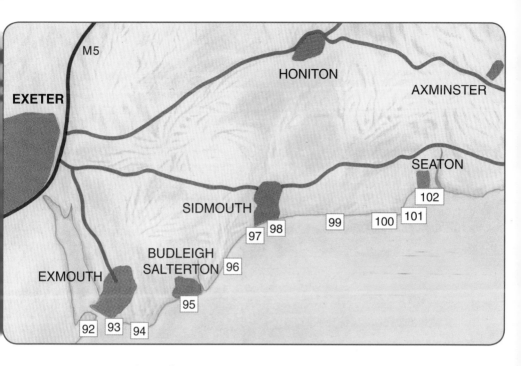

East Devon beaches

Fascinating and dramatic cliff formations form the backdrop to East Devon's beautiful sand and pebble beaches. Geology has made East Devon part of Britain's first natural World Heritage Site: its beaches provide stunning views, not only of the 'Jurassic Coast', which extends east to Studland in Dorset, but westward to Torbay as well.

Aptly named Sandy Bay caters well for families, as does pebbly Seaton, but Exmouth, with 3 km of golden sands, excellent facilities and traditional entertainments, is East Devon's leading family beach. Like Sidmouth and Budleigh Salterton, Exmouth has an attractive promenade and some handsome Georgian buildings dating from its earliest days as a seaside resort.

East of Budleigh Salterton all the beaches are predominantly pebbly, though low tide reveals sand at some. Everywhere there's a steady rhythmic roar, produced by the restless waves as they turn the pebbles and cast them up the beaches. These are not natural harbours, so boats are winched up in numbers, notably at Budleigh's beach, where the plate-sized pebbles are known as 'Budleigh buns', and also at Beer, where many are traditional clinker built fishing boats.

93 Exmouth

With 3 km of golden sands, excellent facilities and traditional entertainments such as donkey rides and Punch and Judy, Exmouth remains very popular with families. Boat trips along the coast and up the Exe are a special feature. Please note parts of the beach are not safe for swimming. Heed warning notices. Deckchair and chalet hire.

P WC ⛺ ✗ ✚ 🐴 🏠 ✗ 🍷

94 Sandy Bay

Sandy Bay lives up to its name, with a long golden beach, ideal for children. There are good facilities in the holiday park, which welcomes day visitors, plus attractions including a museum of country life and farmyard animals. Parking is right by the beach.

P WC ⛺ ✗ ✚ 🐴 🏠 ✗ 🍷 📞

95 Budleigh Salterton

Large pebbles ('Budleigh buns') give this long, steeply shelving beach its character. Budleigh's facilities and the beach are both easily accessible. The Otter Estuary Nature Reserve is at the eastern end. Dogs are permitted at the far western end, which also offers rock pooling, nude bathing and a long vista of cliffs stretching to Torbay.

P WC ⛽ 🐴 🏠 ✗ 🍷 🐦 ℹ️ 🐟

96 Ladram Bay

A predominantly pebbly beach with sand and rock pools at low tide, Ladram Bay has good facilities in the adjacent holiday park and easy access. Boating and diving are popular here and the red sandstone sea stacks, home to many nesting gulls, are a special feature.

97 Jacob's Ladder (Sidmouth)

Like neighbouring Sidmouth this beach consists of pebbles with sand at low tide. It is approached either via steps and a ramp from Connaught Gardens or by the attractive and level Clifton Walkway from Sidmouth. The beach has its own café/shop, and Sidmouth's facilities are only a short walk away. Dogs 🐕 May-September, except at far end of beach. Deckchair hire.

98 Sidmouth Town

Flanked by huge cliffs of red sandstone, Sidmouth's elegant sea front offers a range of facilities and a classic promenade extending to Jacob's Ladder and direct access to the pebble beach. Low tide exposes some sand. Deckchair hire.

99 Weston Mouth

A steepish 1 km walk down the combe is rewarded by the beautiful beach at Weston Mouth. No facilities, but no crowds. Low tide reveals sand below the shingle. This beach is known for nude bathing apart from a small 'textile' area – and the walk back is tough.

100 Branscombe Mouth

Backed by a deep green valley and dramatic high cliffs, Branscombe's long, easily accessed shingle beach with its thatched restaurant is complemented by one of Devon's most attractive villages. The beach as well as Branscombe's working watermill, old bakery and unique thatched forge are maintained by the National Trust.

P WC ⚓ 🐕 🏠 ✕ 🍷 📞

101 Beer

Beer manages to be a delightful family resort, whilst retaining its traditional fishing industry. Fishing boats are winched up on the pebble beach next to the deck chairs, lobster pots and swimmers. Buy fresh fish and shellfish on the spot; take a fishing or a pleasure trip in a Beer boat; or find out more about the locality at the excellent beachside Foundation Centre, with its aquaria, tableaux, video and audio clips.

P WC 🐕 🏠 ✕ 🍷 📞

102 Seaton

Seaton's long pebble beach and 1 km long esplanade afford splendid cliff views east into Dorset and west to Beer Head. If swimming, beware currents near Axmouth. As a traditional family resort, Seaton has ample facilities and is easily accessed. The electric tram ride to historic Colyton via the Axe Valley Nature Reserve is a special attraction.

P WC ➕ 🐕 🏠 ✕ 🍷 🛥 📞 ℹ